Steven Mackey

Busted

for Solo Percussion

Archive Edition

HENDON MUSIC

AN IMAGEM COMPANY

DISTRIBUTED BY

HAL•LEONARD®
CORPORATION
7777 W. BLUEMOUND RD. P.O. BOX 13819 MILWAUKEE, WI 53213

www.boosey.com
www.halleonard.com

INSTRUMENTATION

Timpani in D (32")
3 Tom Toms
Pedal-kick bass drum
Roto Tom Tom tuned to E♭
2 Crotales: D (bottom octave) and E♭ (top octave)
2 Timbales
Vibraslap (mounted on a stend)
Bongos
Small Woodblock
Cow Bell (mounted on a stand)
Small bottle
Referee's Whistle

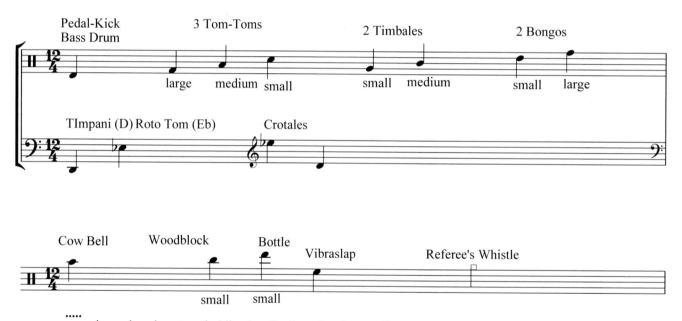

..... = in a relaxed gesture, holding handles loosely, drop mallets and allow them to bounce on drum head.
The bounces should be random, the dots do not indicate the number of bounces.

Medium to edium hard mallets are suggested.

BUSTED

Comissioned by and dedicated to Peggy Benkeser.
Additional editing by Tim Williams.

** Indicates the total number of times that
the passage enclosed in repeat sign is played.

Steven Mackey (2001)

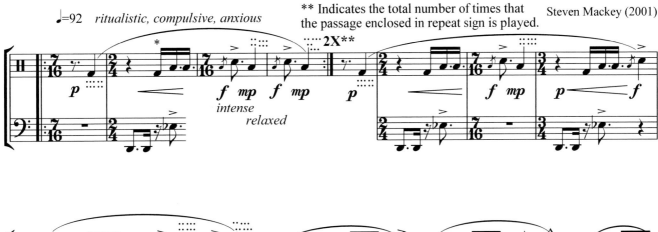

* Special care should be taken with this rhythm: It should have
a "stuttering" feel and should not be "rounded" like a triplet.

4

Move to grace notes slightly, gradually, (almost imperceptibly) earlier...
distance from grace note to main note becomes noticable and grace note.
The performer should "smooth" out the gradual seperation of the two notes
rather than take the increments of the notation too literally.

High Tom remains steady -every 5 1/16th notes.
Low tom, (grace note), gradually moves earlier.
It is more important that the gradually shifting
rhythm leads convincingly to the 1/16th notes
four bars later than to be accurate on each rhythm
along the way is accurate

6

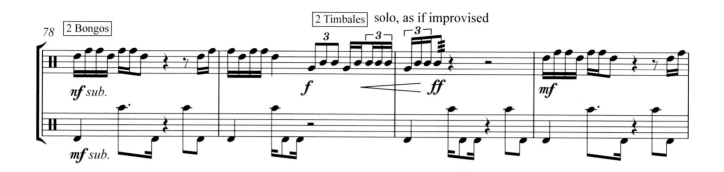

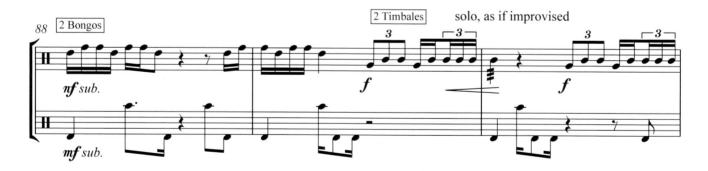

referee's whistle 2nd time only

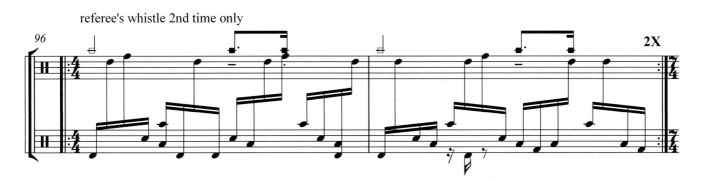

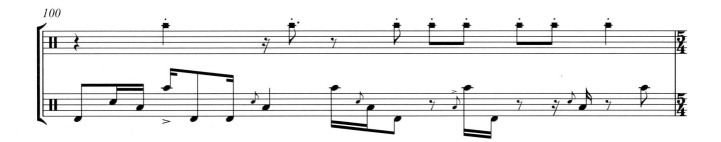

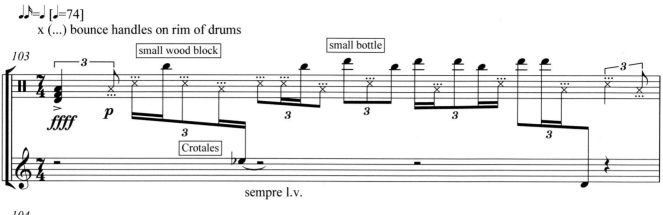

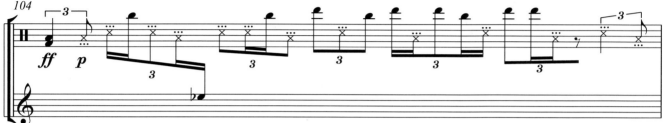

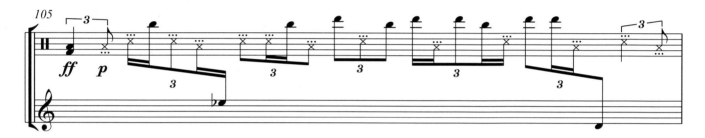

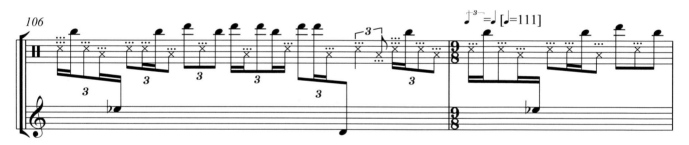

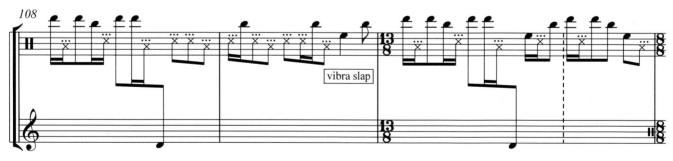

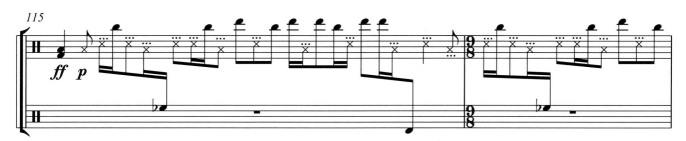

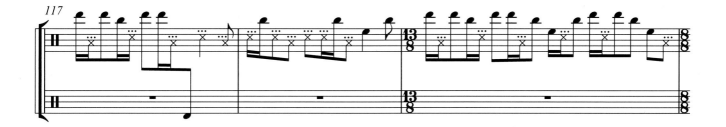

Whistle now soft, merging with
sound of crotales.

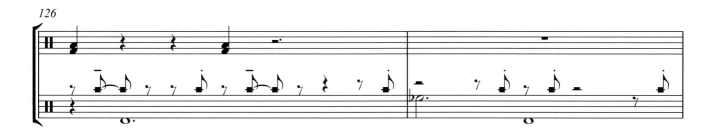